CHANGE

Barack Obama's Plan to Repair the U.S. Economy

Barack Obama

CONTENTS

Statement of Barack Obama on

Emergency Economic Stabilization Legislation

Wednesday, October 1, 2008

WASHINGTON, D.C. - Barack Obama today (Wednesday, October 1, 2008) made the following statement on the Senate floor on the Emergency Economic Stabilization legislation (H.R. 1424), which is being voted on in the Senate later this evening:

As prepared for delivery:

"The fact that we are even here voting on a plan to rescue our economy from the greed and irresponsibility of Wall Street and Washington is an outrage. It is an outrage to every American who works hard and pays their taxes and is doing their best every day to make a better life for themselves and their families. They are angry that Wall Street's mistakes have put their tax dollars at risk, and they should be. I am too.

But while there is plenty of blame to go around and many in Washington and on Wall Street who deserve it, all of us - all of us - have a responsibility to solve this crisis because it affects the financial well-being of every single American. There will be time to punish those who set this fire, but now is the moment for us to come together and put the fire out.

When the House of Representatives failed to act on Monday, we saw the single largest decline of the stock market in two decades. Over one trillion dollars of wealth was lost by the time the markets closed. And it wasn't just the wealth of a few CEOs or Wall Street executives. The 401Ks and retirement accounts that millions count on for their family's future became smaller. The state pension funds of teachers and government employees lost billions upon billions of dollars. Hardworking Americans who invested their nest egg to watch it grow saw it disappear.

But while that decline was devastating, the consequences of the credit crisis that caused it will be even worse if we do not act now.

We are in a very dangerous situation where financial institutions across this country are afraid to lend money. And if all that meant was the failure of a few big banks on Wall Street, it would be one thing.

But that's not what it means. What it means is that if we do not act, it will be harder for Americans to get a mortgage for their home or the loans they need to buy a car or send their children to college. What it means is that businesses won't be able to get the loans they need to open new factories or make payroll for their workers. And if they can't make payroll on Friday, then workers are laid-off on Monday. And then those workers can't pay their bills or pay back their loans to someone else. And it will go and on and on and on, rippling through the entire economy. Thousands of businesses could close. Millions of jobs could be lost. A long and painful recession could follow.

This is not just a Wall Street crisis - it's an American crisis, and it's the American economy that needs this rescue plan. I understand why people would be skeptical when this President asked for a blank check to solve this problem. I was too, and that's why over a week ago, I demanded that this plan include specific proposals to protect the American taxpayer - protections that the Administration eventually agreed to, as well as Democrats and Republicans here in the Senate and over in the House.

First, I said we needed an independent board to provide oversight and accountability for how and where this money is spent at every step of the way.

Second, I said that we cannot help banks on Wall Street without helping the millions of innocent homeowners who are struggling to stay in their homes. They deserve a plan too.

Third, I said that I would not allow this plan to become a welfare program for the Wall Street executives whose greed and irresponsibility got us into this mess.

And finally, I said that if American taxpayers are financing this solution, then they should be treated like investors - they should get every penny of their tax dollars back once this economy recovers.

This last part is important, because it's been the most misunderstood and poorly communicated part of this plan. This is not a plan to just hand over $700 billion of taxpayer money to a few banks. If this is managed correctly, we will hopefully get most or all of our money back, or possibly even turn a profit on the government's investment - every penny of which will go directly back to the American people. And if we fall short, we will levy a fee on financial institutions so that they can repay us for the losses they caused.

Even with all these taxpayer protections, this plan is not perfect. Democrats and Republicans in Congress have legitimate concerns about it. I know many Americans share those concerns. But it is clear that this is what we must do right now to prevent a crisis from turning into a catastrophe. And to the Democrats and Republicans who have opposed this plan, I say - step up to the plate and do what's right for the country, because the time to act is now.

I know many Americans are wondering what happens next. Passing this bill cannot be the end of our work to strengthen our economy - it must be the beginning.

As soon as we pass this rescue plan, we need to move with the same sense of urgency to rescue families on Main Street who are struggling to pay their bills and keep their jobs. I've said it before and I'll say it again: we need to pass an economic stimulus plan that will help folks cope with rising food and gas prices, save one million jobs by rebuilding our schools and roads, and help states and cities avoid budget cuts and tax increases. A plan that would extend expiring unemployment benefits for those Americans who've lost their jobs and cannot find new ones.

We also must do more than this rescue package does to help homeowners stay in their homes. I will continue to advocate bankruptcy reforms to help families stay in their homes and encourage Treasury to study the option of buying individual mortgages like we did successfully in the 1930s. Finally, while we will all hope that this rescue package succeeds, we should be prepared to take more vigorous actions in the months ahead to rebuild capital if necessary.

Just as families are planning for their future in tough times, Washington will have to do the same. Run-away spending and record deficits are not how families run their budgets, and it can't be how Washington handles people's tax dollars. It's time to return to the fiscal responsibility we had in the 1990s. We need to go through the budget, get rid of programs that don't work and make the ones we do need work better and cost less. With less money flowing into the Treasury, some useful programs or policies might need to be delayed in the years ahead.

But there are certain investments in our future that we cannot delay precisely because our economy is in turmoil. We cannot wait to help Americans keep up with rising costs and shrinking paychecks by giving our workers a middle-class tax cut. We cannot wait to relieve the burden of crushing health care costs. We cannot wait to create millions of new jobs by rebuilding our roads and our bridges and investing in the renewable sources of energy that will stop us from sending $700 billion a year to tyrants and dictators for their oil. And we cannot wait to educate the next generation of Americans with the skills and knowledge they need to compete with any workers, anywhere in the world. Those are the priorities we cannot delay.

I won't pretend this will be easy or come without cost. We will all need to sacrifice and we will all need to pull our weight because now more than ever, we are all in this together. What this crisis has taught us is that at the end of the day, there is no real separation between Main Street and Wall Street. There is only the road we're traveling on as Americans - and we will rise or fall on that journey as one nation; as one people.

I know that many Americans are feeling anxiety right now - about their jobs, about their homes, about their life savings. But I also know this - I know that we can steer ourselves out of this crisis. We always have.

During the great financial crisis of the last century, in his first fireside chat, Franklin Roosevelt told his fellow Americans that "..there is an element in the readjustment of our financial system more important than currency, more important than gold, and that is the confidence of the people themselves. Confidence and courage are the essentials of success in carrying out our plan. Let us unite in banishing fear. Together, we cannot fail."

We cannot fail. Not now. This is a nation that has faced down war and depression; great challenges and great threats. And at each and every moment, we have risen to meet these challenges - not as Democrats, not as Republicans, but as Americans. With resolve. With confidence. With that fundamental belief that here in America, our destiny is not written for us, but by us. That's who we are, and that's the country I know we can be right now.

I want to thank the extraordinary leadership of Chairman Dodd and the Banking Committee as well as Chairman Baucus and Majority Leader Reid. I also want to thank the leadership in the House of Representatives.

I urge my colleagues to join me in supporting this important legislation."

Change - Barack Obama's Plan to Repair the U.S. Economy

"Swift Action" on the Economy

Change - Barack Obama's Plan to Repair the U.S. Economy

President-Elect Obama Meets with Economic Advisers, Calls for "Swift Action" on the Economy Friday, November 7, 2008 06:20pm EST /
Barack Obama today held his first press conference as President-Elect to call for "swift action" to fix the nation's economy.

"Immediately after I become president I will confront this economic crisis head-on by taking all necessary steps to ease the credit crisis, help hardworking families, and restore growth and prosperity," President-Elect Obama said.

The press conference followed a private meeting of Obama's Transition Economic Advisory Board, a group of 17 leaders on economic issues that includes former U.S. Treasury Secretaries Robert E. Rubin and Lawrence E. Summers, Google CEO Eric Schmidt and Warren Buffett.

Change - Barack Obama's Plan to Repair the U.S. Economy

24

The 240,000 jobs lost in October marks the tenth consecutive month that our economy has shed jobs. In total we've lost nearly 1.2 million jobs this year and more than 10 million Americans are now unemployed.

Tens of millions of families are struggling to figure out how to pay the bills and stay in their homes. Their stories are an urgent reminder that we are facing the greatest economic challenge of our lifetime, and we're going to have to act swiftly to resolve it.

Now the United States had only one government and one president at a time, and until January 20th of next year, that government is the current administration. I've spoken to President Bush. I appreciate his commitment to ensuring his economic policy team keeps us fully informed as developments unfold, and I'm also thankful for his invitation to the White House.

Immediately after I become president, I'm going to confront this economic crisis head-on by taking all necessary steps to ease the credit crisis, help hard-working families, and restore growth and prosperity.

This morning I met with members of my transition economic advisory board, who are standing behind me alongside my vice president-elect, Joe Biden. They will help to guide the work of my transition team, working with Rohm Emanuel, my chief of staff, in developing a strong set of policies to respond to this crisis. We discussed in the earlier meetings several of the most immediate challenges facing our economy and key priorities on which to focus on in the days and weeks ahead.

First of all, we need a rescue plan for the middle class that invests in immediate efforts to create jobs and provide relief to families that are watching their paychecks shrink and their life savings disappear. A particularly urgent priority is a further extension of unemployment insurance benefits for workers who cannot find work in the increasingly weak economy. A fiscal stimulus plan that will jumpstart economic growth is long overdue. I've talked about it throughout the last few months of the campaign. We should get it done.

Second, we have to address the spreading impact of the financial crisis on the other sectors of our economy, small businesses that are struggling to meet their payrolls and finance their holiday inventories and state and municipal governments facing devastating budget cuts and tax increases. We must also remember that the financial crisis is increasingly global and requires a global response.

The news coming out of the auto industry this week reminds us of the hardship it faces, hardship that goes far beyond individual auto companies to the countless suppliers, small businesses and communities throughout our nation who depend on a vibrant American auto industry.

The auto industry is the backbone of American manufacturing and a critical part of our attempt to reduce our dependence on foreign oil. I would like to see the administration do everything it can to accelerate the retooling assistance that Congress has already enacted. In addition, I've made it a high priority for my transition team to work on additional policy options to help the auto industry adjust, weather the financial crisis and succeed in producing fuel-efficient cars here in the United States of America. And I was glad today to be joined today by Governor Jennifer Granholm, who obviously has great knowledge and great interest on this issue. I've asked my team to explore what we can do under current law and whether additional legislation will be needed for this purpose.

Third. We will review the implementation of this administration's financial program to ensure that the government's efforts are achieving their central goal of stabilizing financial markets while protecting taxpayers, helping homeowners and not unduly rewarding the management of financial firms that are receiving government assistance.

It is absolutely critical that the Treasury work closely with the FDIC, HUD and other government agencies to use the substantial authority that they already have to help families avoid foreclosure and stay in their homes.

Finally, as we monitor and address these immediate economic challenges, we will be moving forward and laying out a set of policies that will grow our middle class and strengthen our economy in the long term. We cannot afford to wait on moving forward on the key priorities that I identified during the campaign including clean energy, health care, education and tax relief for middle-class families.

My transition team will be working on each of these priorities in the weeks ahead, and I intend to reconvene this advisory board to discuss the best ideas for responding to these immediate problems.

Let me close by saying this. I do not underestimate the enormity of the task that lies ahead. We have taken some major action to date, and we will need further action during this transition and subsequent months. Some of the choices that we make are going to be difficult, and I have said before and I will repeat again, it is not going to be quick. It is not going to be easy for us to dig ourselves out of the hole that we are in. But America is a strong and resilient country, and I know we will succeed if we put aside partisanship and politics and work together as one nation. That's what I intend to do.

Change - Barack Obama's Plan to Repair the U.S. Economy

The greatest economic challenge of our lifetime

Change - Barack Obama's Plan to Repair the U.S. Economy

President-elect Obama Calls for Swift Action on the Economy in Weekly Democratic Radio Address Sunday, November 9, 2008 12:15pm EST /
Barack Obama delivered this week's Democratic Radio Address Saturday morning, his first as President-elect.

In the address, President-elect Obama spoke about the need to put partisanship aside to solve the greatest economic challenge of our lifetime.

"Tens of millions of families are struggling to figure out how to pay the bills and stay in their homes," Obama said. "Their stories are an urgent reminder that we are facing the greatest economic challenge of our lifetime, and we must act swiftly to resolve them."

Change - Barack Obama's Plan to Repair the U.S. Economy

On Tuesday, Americans stood in lines that stretched around schools and churches in numbers this nation has never seen. It didn't matter who they were or where they came from, what they looked like or what party they belonged to. They came out and cast their ballot because they believe that in this country our destiny is not written for us but by us.

We should all take pride in the fact that we once again displayed for the world the power of our democracy and reaffirmed the great American deal that this is a nation where anything is possible.

This week I spoke with President Bush, who graciously offered his full support and assistance in this period of transition. Michelle and I look forward to meeting with him and the First Lady on Monday to begin that process. This speaks to a fundamental recognition that here in America we can compete vigorously in elections and challenge each other's ideas yet come together in service of a common purpose once the voting is done. And that is particularly important at a moment when we face the most serious challenges of our lifetime.

Yesterday we woke up to more sobering news about the state of our economy. The 240,000 jobs lost in October marks the tenth consecutive month that our economy has shed jobs. In total we've lost nearly 1.2 million jobs this year and more than 10 million Americans are now unemployed.

Tens of millions of families are struggling to figure out how to pay the bills and stay in their homes. Their stories are an urgent reminder that we are facing the greatest economic challenge of our lifetime, and we must act quickly to resolve them.

In the wake of these disturbing reports, I met with members of my transition economic advisory board team, who will help guide the work of my transition team in developing a strong set of policies to respond to this crisis. Though we must recognize that we only have one president at a time and that President Bush is the leader of our government. I want to ensure that we hit the ground running on January 20th because we don't have a moment to lose.

We discussed several of the most immediate challenges facing our economy and key priorities on which to focus in the days and weeks ahead to ease the credit crisis, help hard-working families, and restore growth and prosperity.

First, we need a rescue plan for the middle class that invests in immediate efforts to create jobs and provides relief to families that are watching their paychecks shrink and their life savings disappear.

Then, we'll address the spreading impact of the financial crisis on other sectors of our economy and ensure that the rescue plan that passed Congress is working to stabilize financial markets while protecting taxpayers, helping homeowners and not unduly rewarding the management of financial firms that are receiving government assistance.

Finally, we will move forward with a set of policies that will grow our middle class and strengthen our economy in the long term. We can't afford to wait on moving forward on the key priorities that I identified during the campaign including clean energy, health care, education and tax relief for middle-class families.

Let me close by saying I do not underestimate the enormity of the task that lies ahead. We've taken some major actions to date, and we will need further actions during this transition and subsequent months. Some of those choices will be difficult, but America is a strong and resilient country. I know that we will succeed if we put aside partisanship and work together as one nation. And that is what I intend to do.

Change - Barack Obama's Plan to Repair the U.S. Economy

Recommended Readings

Barack Obama's Speech on Race : A More Perfect Union

Conscience of a Conservative by Barry Goldwater

The Conservative Mind: From Burke to Eliot by Russell Kirk

How I Made $2,000,000 In The Stock Market by Nicolas Darvas

Technical Analysis of Stock Trends by Robert D. Edwards and John Magee

The Battle For Investment Survival by G. M. Loeb

The Anatomy of Success, Nicolas Darvas

The Dale Carnegie Course on Effective Speaking, Personality Development, and the Art of How to Win

Friends & Influence People, Dale Carnegie

The Law of Success In Sixteen Lessons by Napoleon Hill
(Complete, Unabridged), Napoleon Hill

It Works, R. H. Jarrett,

The Art of Public Speaking (Audio CD), Dale Carnegie

The Success System That Never Fails (Audio CD), W.
Clement Stone

BN Publishing
Improving People's Life

www.bnpublishing.net